A Dot Markers & Paint Daubers Kids Activity Book

Learn as you play: Do a dot page a day

Cute Bugs

14 Peaks Creative Arts

Fly

SLUG

Honey Bee

ANTS

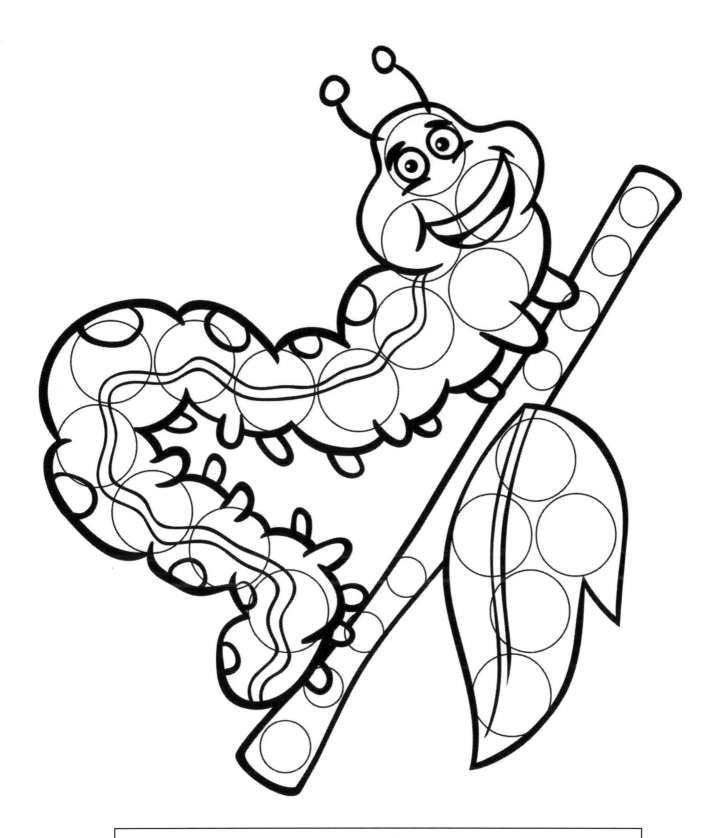

CATERPILLAR

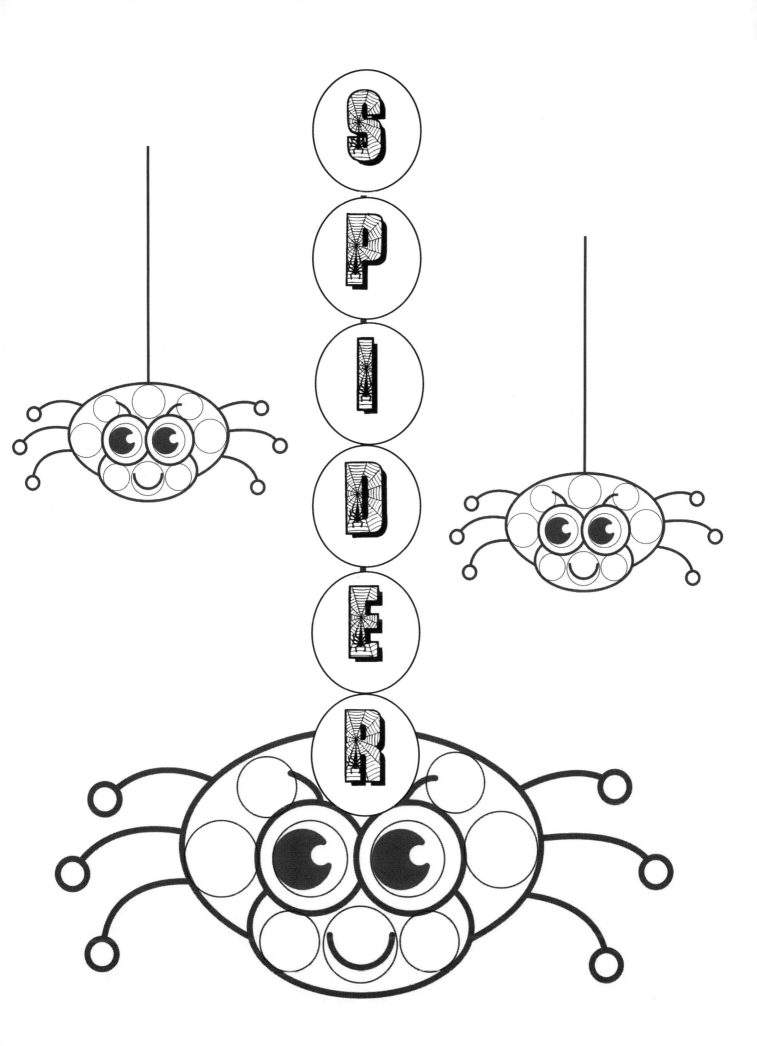

Butterfly

Inch Worm

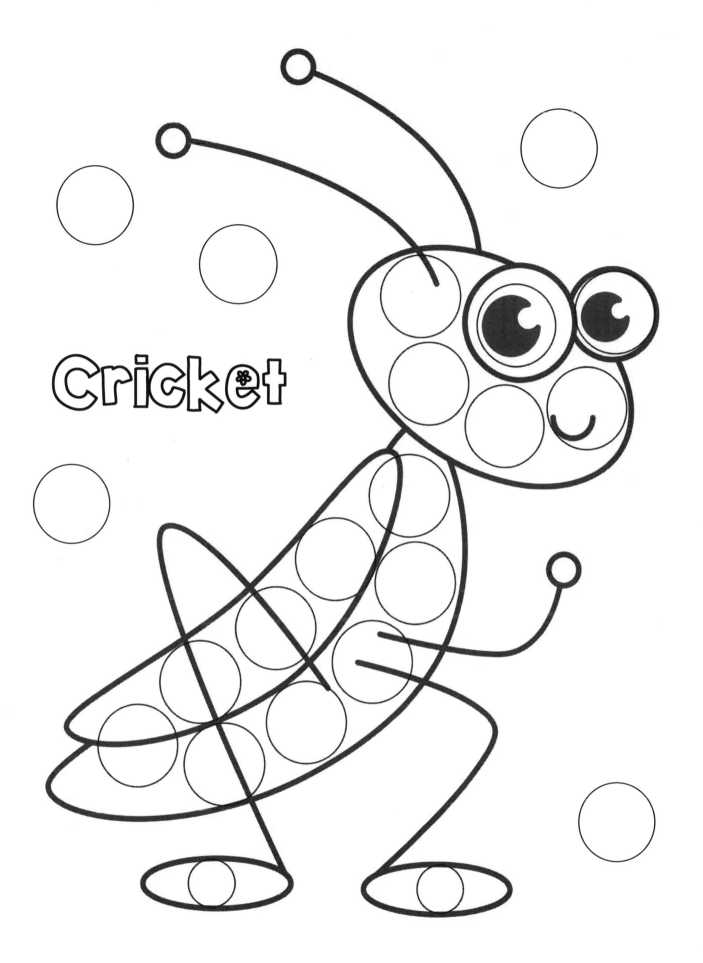

Cricket

Butterfly

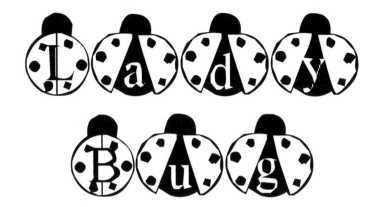

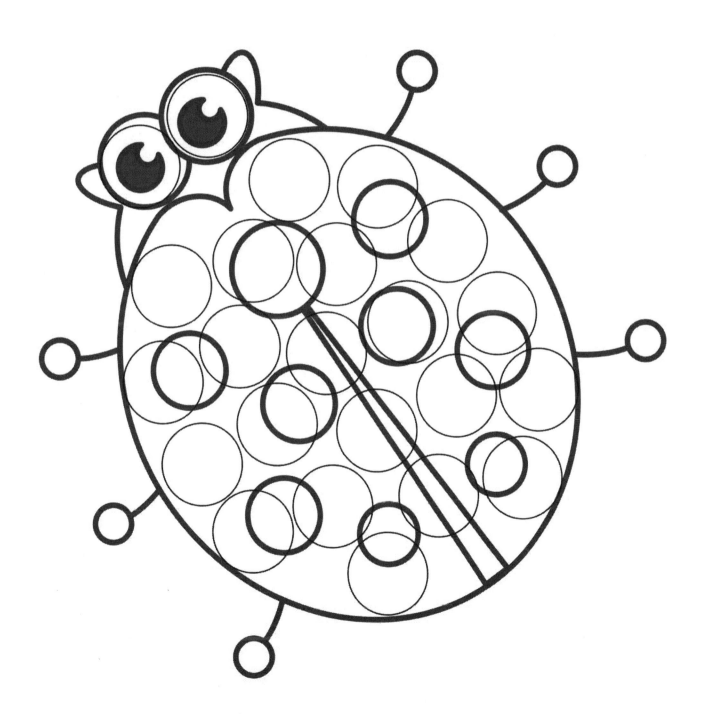

BEETLE

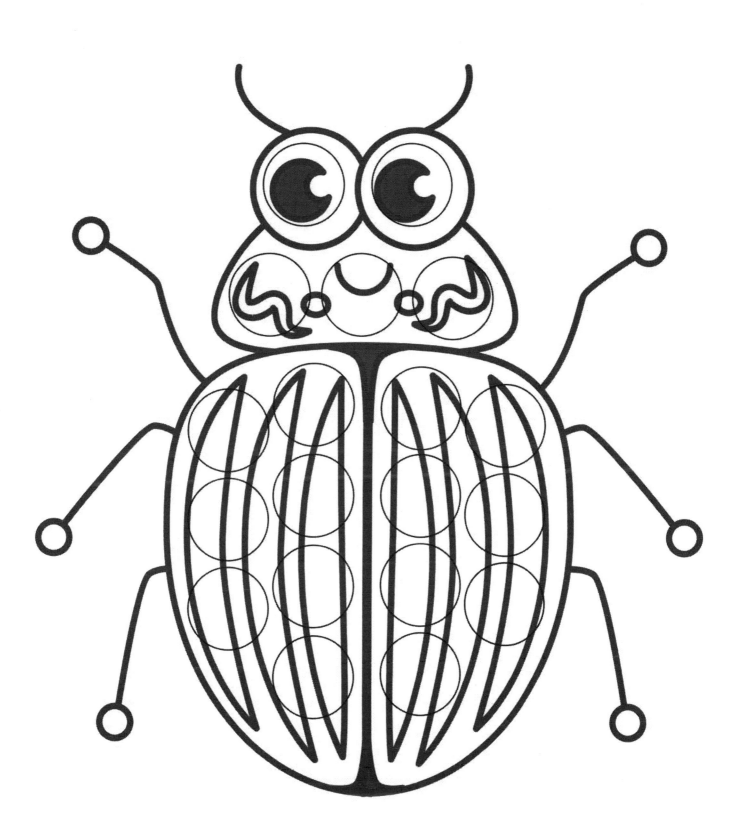

SCORPION

ANT

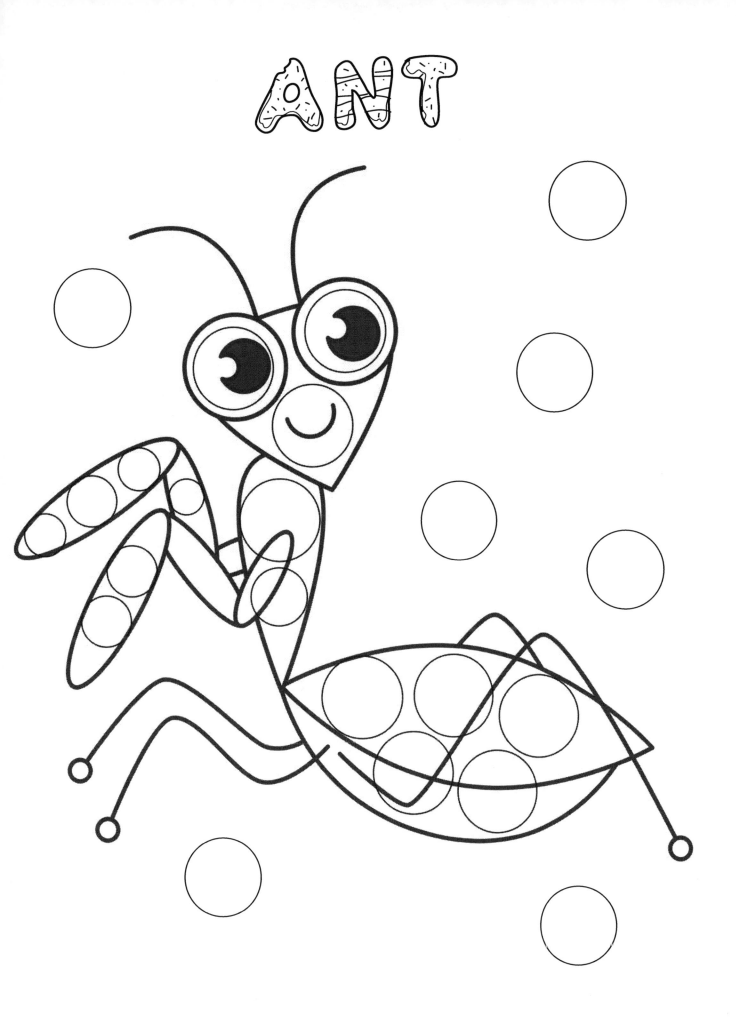

LADY BUG

Bumble bee

caterpillar

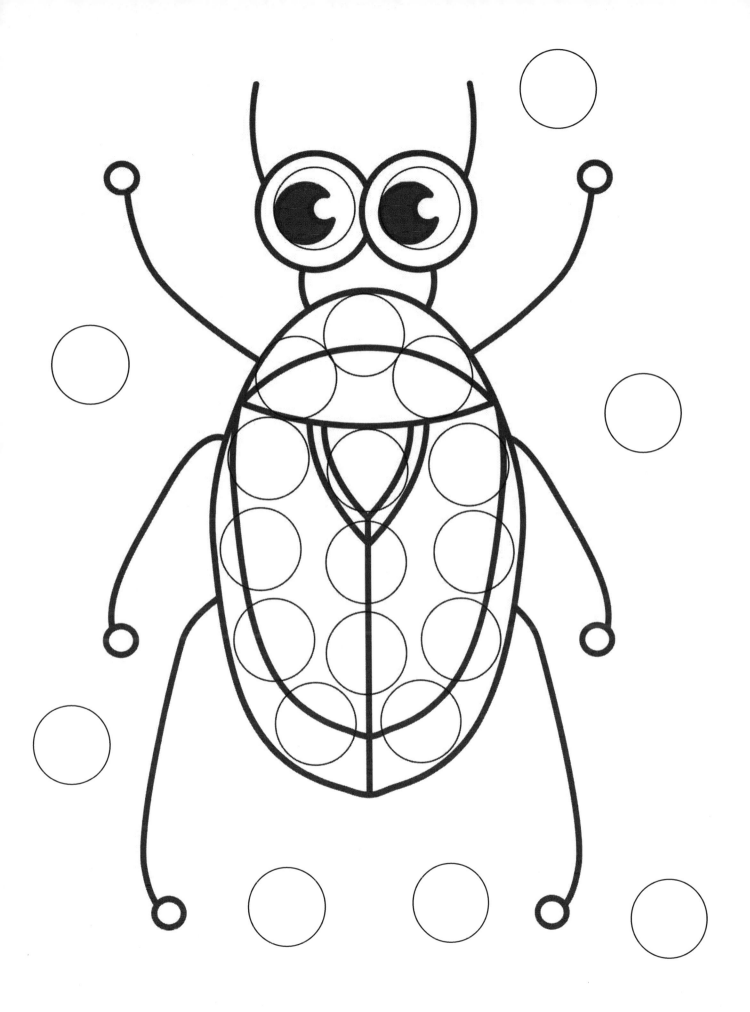

slug

Rhinoceroses
Beetle

Excerpt from our Dot Marker Book

Animal Faces

Exclusively on Amazon

Excerpt from our Series

Numbers with Animals

Exclusively on Amazon

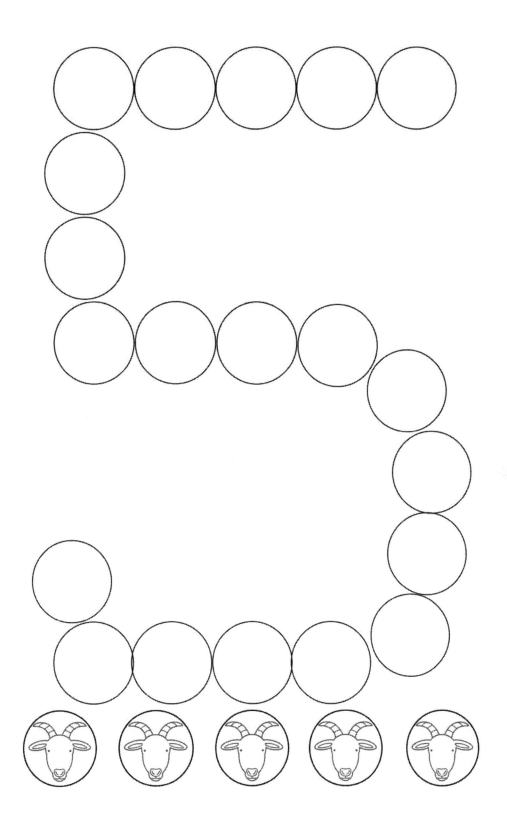

Excerpt from our Dot Marker Book

Construction Dots

Exclusively on Amazon

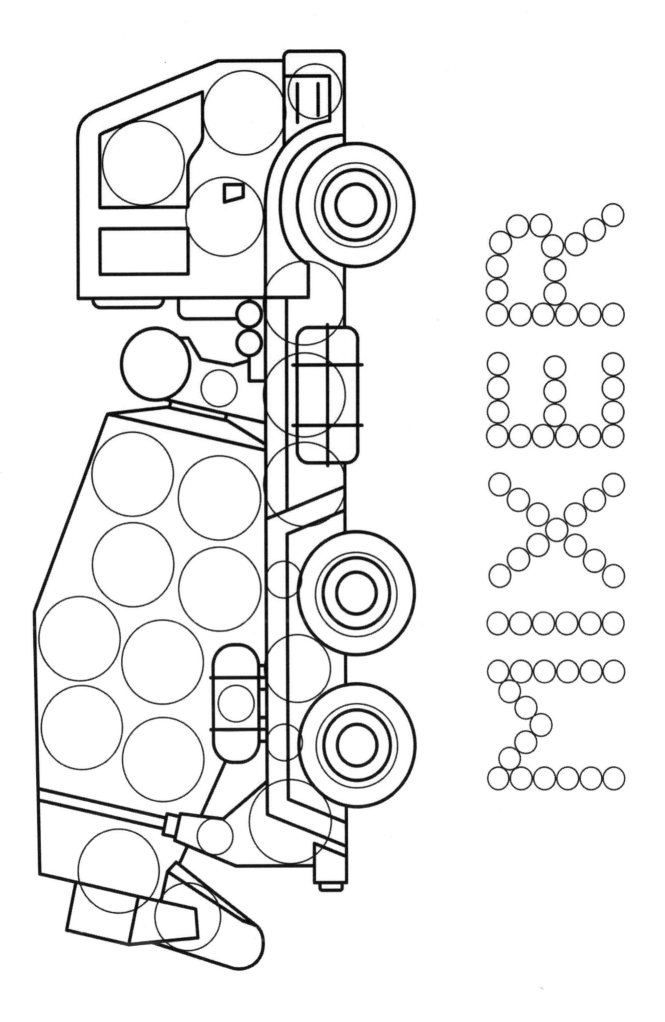

www.14-peaks.com

Find more of our books exclusively on amazon.

Dot Marker Series

Silly Scents Series

Made in the USA
Lexington, KY
31 August 2018